Penny —
More favorite
for a favorite

Christmas '95

Love,
Frankie

MAASAI

PEOPLE OF CATTLE

DAVID M. ANDERSON

TRIBAL WISDOM

CHRONICLE BOOKS
SAN FRANCISCO

A Labyrinth Book

First published in the United States in 1995 by Chronicle Books.

Design by Generation Associates

The Little Wisdom Library —Tribal Wisdom was produced by Labyrinth Publishing (UK) Ltd.

Printed and bound in Italy by L.E.G.O.

Library of Congress Cataloging-in-Publication Data: Anderson, David,

1957 - Maasai: people of cattle / by David M. Anderson. p. cm.

ISBN 0–8118–0831–9

1. Maasai (African people) — Social life and customs.   1. Title

DT433.545.M33A47 1995

308.4'089965—dc20   94-40060

                                                                                    CIP

Distributed in Canada by Raincoast Books,
8680 Cambie Street, Vancouver, B.C. V6P 6M9
10 9 8 7 6 5 4 3 2 1

Chronicle Books

275 Fifth Street, San Francisco, CA 94103

Introduction

The figure of the Maasai warrior, perched on one leg to gaze across the savannah with a long-bladed spear in his hand while tending his cattle, has become the quintessential international image of East Africa in the late twentieth century. Postcards, T-shirts, and tourist company logos of all varieties convey the Maasai as the stereotype of a traditional, even backward people, who show haughty disdain for the ways of the West. For many the Maasai have come to epitomize the romantic dignity of the "noble savage" in a fast vanishing world.

It would be easy to believe that this image was merely the product of the commodification of the Maasai with the rise of tourism in East Africa. Kenya has one of the most successful tourist sectors in the world, and it is undeniably true that the Maasai have been "marketed" to the great benefit of the country's tourist industry since gaining independence from British colo-

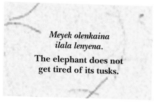

Meyek olenkaina ilala lenyena.

The elephant does not get tired of its tusks.

Page 4: A Maasai herdsman and his cattle.
Cattle are highly prized possessions and bring prestige to their owner.
Page 7: A young Maasai woman wearing the elaborate bead jewelry for which the Maasai are famous.
Page 8: A young Maasai *moran* (warrior) blows a Kudu horn.
Opposite: Three Maasai *moran* performing a dance in their *manyatta*.

nial rule in 1963. The Tanzanian government, keen to capitalize upon the tourist potential, is now rapidly following suit.

Yet the image of the conservative and disdainful Maasai has deeper historical roots. Back in the late 1940s, when other parts of East Africa were beginning to be more rapidly developed, one despairing colonial official among the Maasai lamented their conservatism and lack of interest in modernization, describing himself as "the curator of the Maasai museum." Earlier European writers also noted the insularity of the Maasai, even predicting that their unwillingness to adapt in a changing world would lead to their extinction within a few generations. One European writer even entitled his

book *The Last of the Maasai*, believing that their demise was imminent.

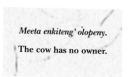

Meeta enkiteng' olopeny.

The cow has no owner.

These expressions of cultural value reflected the prevailing European intellectual currents of their time. Most nineteenth century European observers tended to see Maasai society in terms of social Darwinism. By this reasoning, Maasai and other herding peoples were less civilized than agriculturists, whose form of production demanded a sedentary lifestyle and a more developed use of technology, yet more advanced than hunters, who culled an existence from the wild.

It was supposed that with the advance of civilization, all societies would move toward sedentary agriculture: Maasai commitment to cattle herding, and to the nomadic pastoralist lifestyle that necessarily accompanied it upon the plains of East Africa, had no place in the modern world.

Such dire predictions of the demise of the Maasai way of life have proved to be premature. Maasai culture and society has been more resilient to change than probably any other in East Africa. In this sense, conservatism has been a strength, for the Maasai have been unwilling to lightly discard their own social values. The Maasai age-set system, their family structure, their ritual and symbolic rites, and their own sense of cultural identity have all been sustained through to the end of the twentieth century in forms similar to those of one hundred years ago.

Opposite : A young Maasai *moran* looking after his cattle. He is pictured here in Tanzania. *Above :* A Maasai bull inside the *moran manyatta* where the herds are guarded and the young warriors live.

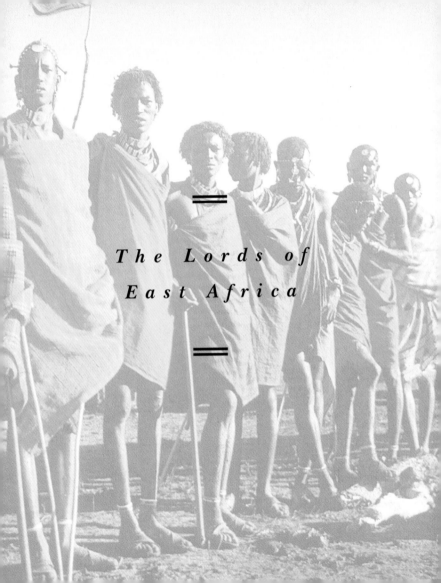

The Lords of East Africa

The Maasai dominated the plains between Lake Victoria and the coast of East Africa in the nineteenth century. The first stories that Europeans at the coast heard of the Maasai was of a fierce and warmongering people. Maasai raiding parties reputedly preyed upon their neighbors, carrying off livestock and women and slaughtering men. The warriors of Maasai, the *moran*, were the most feared in East Africa. This image of predation has endured as part of the stereotypical picture of the Maasai long after they ceased to dominate the region.

Like all such stereotypes, the nineteenth-century image of the warlike Maasai was exaggerated. Behind their image as "the Lords of East Africa" lay a more complex truth. During the mid-nineteenth century the Maasai had fallen to squabbling amongst themselves over cattle, pastures, and water.

Ironically, this situation was a product of their successful utilization of the rangeland environment. As Maasai pastoralists became increasingly rich in cattle, so the competition for grazing and water became more intense. It was the struggles between Maasai sections for control of environmental resources that provoked much of the warfare in the region that Europeans heard about.

There are now about sixteen separate named sections of the Maasai, each inhabiting their own discrete territories. These sections, as they now appear, are largely the result of the wars and struggles of the nineteenth century. In this process, some previously existing sections, such as Laikipiak, disappeared, being defeated and absorbed by others, while sections such as Purko and Kisongo were enlarged.

All Maasai sections speak the Maa language, although with differences in dialect from north to south. And all are recognizably Maasai in their material culture, most vividly characterized by the distinctive embroidered beadwork worn predominantly by the women. But when one examines their communities more closely, it becomes apparent that there are differences in the details of culture and practice from one section to the next. The anthropologist Paul Spencer, a fluent Maa speaker with long experience of Maasai society, has explained these differences as part of a historical process. The Maasai moved south, into the plains of the Rift Valley in what is now central Kenya and northern Tanzania, only in the eighteenth century. As some sections of Maasai gradually moved further south, their social organization became more complex, with variations emerging between sections. This unfolding pattern is part of the dynamic reality of Maasai society, a society in which continuity and change are both strongly evident.

Meikitikitoyu oloota esumash.
**You cannot tickle a hungry person.
(He would not laugh).**

Similarly, while the Maasai are commonly presented as a people who hold their cultural and individual independence in high regard, their society is in fact

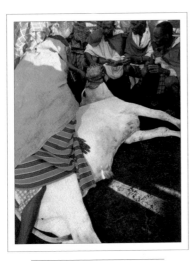

firmly bound by ties of dependence—the dependence of sons upon their fathers, of husbands upon their wives, and of age-mates upon one another. This can also be seen in relationships between different Maasai sections. Although they express themselves culturally in terms of cattle, the truth is that many Maasai are not pastoralists at all, but farmers and hunters.

The image of the Maasai as a people who consume only meat, milk, and blood is nothing more than a mythical ideal. The plains herders have always depended upon the cultivators to supplement their diet. And there have always been Maasai communities that cultivate, such as the community at Arusha in northern Tanzania today. Here, and at other

Page 14: Maasai *moran* at an initiation ceremony that will take them into manhood. The event is now becoming rarer.
Previous pages: A Maasai *moran* blows a Kudu horn to symbolize his age-grade's coming of age.
Above: A cow is shown here being ritually slaughtered by suffocation to prevent wasting the blood that the Maasai drink.

settlements along the escarpments of the Rift Valley, Maa speaking herders and farmers have been able to exchange their produce. At some of these settlements, Maa speakers have employed well-designed irrigation canals to draw water from the escarpment gorges to water their fields. It is ironic that the Maasai, stereotyped as the proud pastoralists of the plains, should also be numbered among the most sophisticated agricultural technologists of Eastern Africa.

Throughout the Rift Valley of Kenya and Tanzania, the barriers between hunting, cultivating, and herding are best understood as permeable membranes, through which people must pass from time to time in order to survive. During drought and famine, or other times of misfortune, a herder who loses cattle might seek refuge with a neighboring community of Maasai cultivators, or might even become a *Dorobo*, that is, take up hunting in the forests. Although such alternatives are often despised in the normative description of ideal Maasai society, they are at the same time understood as well established and necessary strategies for survival. Only in this way has Maasai culture sustained itself so well in the capricious environment of the East African savannah, where drought or cattle disease might very rapidly decimate a family's wealth.

Above: Maasai men in a *moran manyatta.* Men grow up together, establishing
strong bonds that usually last a lifetime.

People of Cattle

Previous pages: Maasai herds are seen here near the
holy forest in the Loita Hills, in southern Kenya.
The Maasai respect and manage the forest themselves.
Above: Maasai *moran* gather together during their
coming into manhood ceremony.

aasai are "people of cattle." Their culture is dominated by cattle, as are their social relationships, their ritual and ceremonial life, their symbolism, and even the idioms of their language. This is as true for those Maa speakers who farm as for those who herd.

But to say that Maasai have a ritual and cultural attachment to cattle is to tell only part of the story. At the heart of their respect for cattle lie strong economic and ecological truths. On the dry grasslands of Eastern Africa cattle offer security where agriculture alone cannot. Maasai cattle pastoralism is well adapted to the environment of the plains. The rainfall of the plains is too little and too irregular for sustainable cultivation of cereals. One year in five might bring drought. And every person will live to see a prolonged and catastrophic drought—a drought that will kill. In such a land, the mobility of pastoralism is essential. An understanding of ecology, and of the landscape of the Rift Valley, is the crucial element of Maasai existence. As herders of cattle and shepherds of goats and sheep, Maasai must move between seasonal grazing areas and watering points, occupying the drier lowlands in the wet season and staying in the higher, wetter areas when the weather is dry. Deciding when to move, and in which direction, is the herd owner's responsibility, and the

prosperity of the family will hang on this decision. A bad decision during a drought may see a herd of eighty or more reduced to less than thirty animals. It is not surprising, therefore, that the physical environment forms such a central element in Maasai perceptions. The symbolic geography of this landscape is redolent in the variety of Maasai place names that refer to the quality or type of grazing, the purity and freshness of water, and the general suitability of an area to the pursuit of pastoralism. The success of every herder hinges upon his knowledge of the landscape, its ecology, and his livestock.

The value of cattle is also judged in social terms. There are good

reasons for this. To spread his risk, and so increase his security, a wise herder will distribute his animals among relatives, age-mates, and friends. Livestock are given in loans and bonds, to transact marriages, and in payment of a variety of social debts. If disaster should strike his main herd, the prudent herder can at least hope to call in debts and obligations from others in order to begin rebuilding. In a single lifetime it is not unusual for a Maasai household to have to build and then rebuild a substantial herd two or three times. So it is that while Maasai set high store by the independence of the individual, their dependence upon others is very tangible.

The incursions of the modern world have raised new challenges for the Maasai in retaining a viable system of pastoralism. Farmers look for profitable opportunities to cultivate upland seasonal grazing lands, and national parks, set up for the protection of wildlife, have often been carved out at the cost of restricting Maasai access to pasture and water. In Amboseli, the Serengeti, and especially in the Ngorongoro Crater (designated as a World Heritage Site), local Maasai communities have sometimes found themselves at odds with the desires of conservationists. Attempts to redirect income to the Maasai from the parks and from tourism have been made, but with limited success. To those who argue for the exclusion of Maasai pastoralists from the areas reserved for wildlife, there is an answer in the ample historical and archaeological evidence of the coexistence of both. The present ecology of the savannah has been shaped by the actions of pastoralists as much as by wildlife.

Previous pages: Maasai *moran* and cattle inside a *moran* village.
Opposite: A *moran* carries reeds to be laid under a bull which will be ritually slaughtered for their initiation into manhood.

Emutai —
The Time of
Disasters

The importance of ecology to Maasai society echoes through all aspects of their folklore. Droughts, famines, and epidemics among the cattle are the events which calibrate the past and haunt the future. The modern history of the Maasai is dominated by the memory of Emutai—the time of disasters. It was at this time, during the last two decades of the nineteenth century, that many Maasai lost their vast herds of cattle and became temporarily impoverished. This weakening of their former strength and dominance in the Rift Valley was the immediate prelude to the European conquest of East Africa. The poignancy of Emutai has been intensified in Maasai oral history by its identification with the arrival of Europeans, and the dramatic changes that brought.

Emutai was in fact a series of epidemiological disasters, rushing in, one upon the other. First, bovine pleuro-pneumonia attacked the Maasai herds. Then they were devastated by rinderpest—the worst cattle plague that they had then known. Over a matter of months rinderpest smote herd after herd. The infection was spread by wild animals who grazed the same pastures as well as by apparently healthy cattle who would, suddenly and without warning, succumb to the disease. By then it was usually too late to save the rest of the herd. Rinderpest was a disease the Maasai had not known before in the nineteenth century. There was, in fact, little they could have done to isolate herds and prevent the spread of infection. But their task was made no easier by outbreaks of smallpox, which ravaged the human population in the wake of the rinderpest. Smallpox was introduced at this time along the expanding commercial trade routes into the East African interior from the coast. A severe famine added to their misery at the end of the 1890s, by which time Maasai sections were struggling for survival against one another in what amounted to a civil war. Emutai truly was a time of disasters.

The oral histories of Maasai families are replete with accounts of their struggle for survival during Emutai. The resources of Maasai pastoralism were stretched to the breaking point, and Maasai refugees inundated their farming and hunting neighbors. It was at a time such as Emutai that Maasai

Previous pages: Maasai *moran* coat their heads with red ochre after their hair is shaved, signifying manhood.
Above: Young Maasai children help with the herds. Here a young boy is shown looking after a herd of goats.

fell back upon their carefully constructed social networks of dependence and reciprocity.

In times of trouble such as Emutai, the Maasai also seek guidance from their diviners, the *loibon*. Diviners have the potential to work for good or evil, and are accordingly both feared and respected by Maasai. They are commonly consulted when sorcery is suspected, but in the midst of drought or epidemic they play a more prominent role in rain-making and in healing the land.

The most important diviners among the Maasai all claim to descend from the same Looki-dongi family, and among them are some who are attributed with wider powers of prophecy. At the time of Emutai, two brothers of the Lookidongi dynasty, Sentue and Lenana, emerged as rivals, and their dispute fuelled the cattle raiding of Maasai sections against one another. Diviners, and especially prophets, remain important and powerful public figures among the Maasai today.

Opposite: A Maasai *moran* bites into the lungs and heart of a ritually slaughtered bull as part of his initiation into manhood.

Above : A young Maasai *moran* standing
guard over his herd.

Matapato Maasai War Song

I the warrior with the long thin spear

Am not at all arrogant

But a humble being whose neck is weighed down by poverty,

Poverty of a herd that falls below fifty,

A herd that is despised by the girl who milks

As well as by the boy who herds,

A herd that does not finish a mere foot of a tree

When it is lush with vegetation.

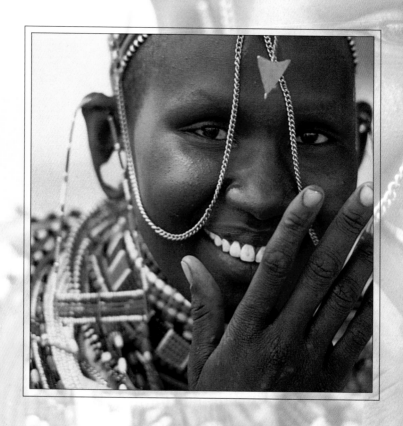

The Gifts of God

Maasai spirituality is expressed through cultural practice rather than through an adherence to any clear religious philosophy. For this reason, Maasai spiritual beliefs can seem elusive and are difficult to define precisely. Yet the Maasai show a great awareness of the powerful, invisible forces of their universe. The elements, especially rain, thunder, and lightning, are viewed as gifts or punishments, signs of the greater force shaping the earth. When the Maasai speak of "god," they use the name Engai, and this word can also be applied to rain and thunder. Men and women often give up prayers to Engai in the hope of good fortune and blessings. Engai is the spiritual force which governs the universe.

The cultural values and beliefs which underlie Maasai spirituality are not neatly summarized in written words. Rather, it is the spoken word that conveys the essence of Maasai culture. The recollection of oral histories, storytelling, the singing of songs, and the recital of poetry are all vehicles for the transmission of culture from one generation to the next. Maasai oral culture is thus a dynamic, changing stream. And even in the language of everyday conversation, the heavy use of proverb and analogy is used to reflect many of the elements of what it is to be Maasai. The

Previous pages: A beautiful young woman, elaborately adorned in the Maasai fashion, hides her face shyly behind her hand.

A Maasai Blessing

May beer nurture the elders,
Those who drank and those who smelled it.
May it nurture them all.
May it nurture the women;
Make us bear on hides without holes.
God, make us elders.
May the calves fill the pens,
May the cattle fill the homesteads,
May the children play at the hearth.
Tell the fire to stay burning.
Let it eat the ritual meats.

cultural context of Maasai spirituality can be clearly seen in this typical blessing, chanted in the form of a prayer on the previous page.

Maasai myths and traditions are passed on to children through storytelling, both as a means of entertainment in the family home during the evening, and as a way of conveying the values and structures of Maasai life. Stories are highly durable vehicles for cultural symbolism.

Left: A detail of an earring. The Maasai are famous for their intricate beadwork, and nowadays often sell it commercially.
Opposite: Maasai *moran* have fat smeared on their foreheads as part of their initiation ceremony.

Among these myths are many stories about god, or, to be more precise, the gods, for the Maasai believe there have been two gods, the black god and the red god. The story of the black god and the red god was first written down by a European in the early years of this century and has been recorded in much the same form many times since:

There are two gods, a black one and a red one. The black god is good and the red one malicious. One day the black god said to the red one: "Let us give the people some water, for they are dying of hunger." The red god agreed, and made the rain come heavily. After a time the red god told the black god to stop the rain, as enough had fallen. But the black god refused, saying the people had not had enough. So the rain

continued to the next morning, when the black god made it stop. A few days later the black god noticed that the grass was again very dry, and proposed they should give the people more water. But the red god refused to make the rain come. At this, the gods quarreled, and the red god threatened to kill all the people. Since then the black god protects the people and lives near to them, with the red god above him. When the thunder crashes in the heavens, it is the red god trying to come to earth to kill the people.

God thus represents the power of the elements to shape the environment of the plains to bring or deny the rain that will nurture the grass to feed the cattle and water the *shamba* (farm) to grow the crops. The two gods, black and red, are often seen to represent Maasai notions of good and evil, or (more prosaically) good fortune and bad luck.

Other myths explain the ordering of the world, and especially the position of the

Maasai as herders of cattle. In a story that expresses the cultural superiority of pastoralism over other ways of life, we learn how it was that the Maasai came to have the ownership of cattle as the gift of god:

One day god told Maasinta, the first Maasai, to build a large kraal (a cattle enclosure). Maasinta did this. Next, god told him to go and stand inside his house, and not to make a sound, no matter what happened. Very early the next morning, Maasinta heard a

Opposite: Cattle stockades in the Loita Hills in southern Kenya. This is a region where the Maasai can still maintain their traditional way of life. *Above:* Maasai *moran* enter their dwelling in the village they have to spend a year in prior to becoming men.

sound like thunder. God had lowered a long leather thong from the skies, and down this thong, into the kraal, came cattle. There were so many cattle, and their noise was so great, that the surface of the earth shook. Maasinta was gripped by fear, but he did not cry out. But while the cattle were still descending, the Dorobo *(the hunter) who lived with Maasinta woke up from his sleep and went outside to see what all the noise was. He screamed out in surprise. On hearing his cry, god cut the thong and stopped the cattle descending. Thinking it was Maasinta who had cried out and disobeyed his instruction, god told him he would receive no more cattle, but would have to care for those that were now on the earth.*

Here the *Dorobo* has acted foolishly and so prevented the creation of more cattle. So it is that there are only enough cattle for the herder Maasai, and the *Dorobo* and others must live without cattle.

Several mythical stories feature the character Naiteru-kop—literally, "the beginner of the earth"—who is portrayed as the divine intermediary between the black god and man. Naiteru-kop was unwittingly made the harbinger of death but only because the foolishness of man led to the misunderstanding of his instructions:

Leeyio was the first man Naiteru-kop brought to earth. Naiteru-kop told him:

Opposite: Maasai girls, dressed in their finest jewelry, watch closely during the young men's initiation ceremony.

46

"When a man dies and you dispose of the corpse you must remember to say, man die and come back again, moon die and remain away." So, when it happened that a neighbor's child died, Leeyio was summoned to dispose of the body. But when he took the body outside he made a mistake, saying: "Moon die and come back again, man die and stay away." After that, all men were doomed to die.

Maasai social organization is based upon the idea of the age-grade. The movement of a person from one age-grade to the next marks the most important transition in the life of an individual and in the wider life of the community. Age-grades are linked to the rites of passage from childhood to adolescence and from adolescence to full adulthood as elders of the community.

These processes of change are measured in a cycle of approximately fifteen years duration, this being the interval between successive age-grades. The name given to each male age-grade when they reach the stage of *moran* (adolescents and warriors) frames any Maasai notions of time and history. In recounting any event

Nailoikino motioo kima.

Pots take turns to sit on the fire.

from the past, an elder will invariably allude to it having taken place during the period when that named age-grade were *moran.* Age-grades, and all of the ceremonies associated with them, are then the crucial markers of the Maasai life-cycle.

The ceremonies of circumcision and clitoridectomy mark the opening of an age-grade. Although these ritual operations are now the subject of much controversy in East Africa and elsewhere, they still form an important part of Maasai culture. Traditional

Maasai beliefs link clitoridectomy with fertility, and a woman who has not undergone the operation will find it difficult to marry among Maasai. These rites of passage are also important for the transmission of Maasai values from one generation to the next. Education in Maasai culture and wisdom forms a major part of the rituals associated with circumcision and clitoridectomy.

Feasts take place to celebrate all these rites of passage through a person's life cycle, from birth to death. It is usually only on these

Previous pages: A young Maasai child eagerly drinks a bowl of milk. Cow's milk is highly valued by the Maasai. *Opposite:* Maasai gourds filled with milk and honey beer that will be consumed during the *moran's* initiation ceremony.

occasions that cattle are slaughtered to be eaten, although the meat of sheep and goats forms a regular part of the Maasai diet. All public celebrations provide opportunities to reinforce the symbolic values of Maasai culture.

At a meat feast these values are reflected in the choice of the color of the animal to be slaughtered—some colors and hide patterns are thought to be more propitious than others. The distribution of the various cuts of meat also has significance. Certain parts of the animal are attributed high prestige and symbolic value and go to senior male elders; other cuts are considered to give strength to the *moran*, and others are deemed more suitable for consumption by women. It is the responsibility of a good host to ensure that the meat at any feast is distributed appropriately.

Meye olororita modiok.
He that steps on cow dung does not die.

The most important of all the Maasai ceremonies is the *eunoto*, at which the *moran* of one age-grade leave their *manyatta*—the separate camp where as *moran* they remained aloof from ordinary family life—to become full elders, to marry wives, and to establish themselves as household heads and fathers. The bonds linking the men of one age-grade together are very strong, and it is very likely that a person's lifelong companions and closest friends will be others of the same age-grade.

In any age-grade system, gerontocratic principles tend to predominate: elders have more power and authority than younger men, and there are inevitable tensions between the generations. Each age-grade must conform to the rules of the Maasai society, but at the same time each age-set is thought to be unique. Just as a parent may marvel at the development of a child who learns to talk or walk, although of course every child acquires these skills, so it is that Maasai communities will constantly speculate and debate the progress of a particular age-set: how will its members turn out? What characteristics will they manifest in dealing with the challenges of life? How will they cope with the transitions from boyhood to *moran*hood and eventually elderhood? There is a set pattern to this cycle of life that is predictable, yet within that pattern there is an infinite possibility of variation.

Olapa oibor inkera.
Children are the bright moon.

The Maasai age-set system gives their society its structure, but the family is the arena in which the dramas of daily life take place. As polygamy is the norm, family relationships can be complex and sometimes tense. The role of the father as a caring patriarch is emphasized, but it is through the labors and commitment of the wives that family harmony is secured. In the words of Telelia Chieni, an elderly woman of Matapato Maasai: "It is the men, of course, who control things, but the women do not mind, for they do not want to interfere in matters that belong to the men.... I do know the woman's business about looking after her family, and I do know how to bear children. I can do all the work. All the Maasai have their work to do. This includes the wives and the children they bear and the celebrations after children are born."

To the untrained eye a Maasai homestead, like the one in which Telelia lives, has a random and somewhat chaotic appearance. In fact, life within the thorn enclosure that surrounds every homestead is regulated in a well established pattern. Several families will share a single homestead, but each will have its own gate. Wives build their huts to the side of the family cattle gate, in a strict alternation—the first wife to the right-hand side of the entrance, the second wife to the left-hand side, the third to the right, and so on. The low, rectangular houses are built with wooden poles and saplings, intertwined with grasses and plastered with cow dung, the entrance always facing the center of the enclosure. Inside the house, space is also clearly defined, with sleeping areas for different members of the family. Everything has its place.

Opposite: A Maasai woman coats her family hut with cow dung, an example of how cows supply more than milk and meat.

Children are much valued, and deeply loved among all Maasai. A birth is widely celebrated and any misfortune to befall a child causes distress to the whole community. They are the future and there is a very palpable sense in which all Maasai recognize this. Children are, quite literally, seen as the measure of the success and well-being of the Maasai. *"Olapa oibor inkera"* ("Children are the bright moon") is a popular Maasai proverb. To die without children is thought to be a terrible fate.

The cycle of life, as the story of Naiteru-kop and Leeyio reminds us, must inevitably end with death. There is no Maasai belief in an afterlife, but the establishment and perpetuation of a family through the prosperity of its chil-dren is a goal that all strive to achieve. It offers an immortality of sorts.

The respectful treatment of the dead is a very important ritual for the family concerned, for the corpse is thought to be a powerful pollutant and anyone who fails to behave appropriately at the time of a death risks a curse or evil fortune. Today, as one of the few concessions to the presence of Christian missions in their midst, it is usual for Maasai to discreetly bury their dead. But in the past the body would be laid to rest under the shade of a tree, to be left there for the hyenas to devour at night. In the rituals of death, as in life, the physicality of the Maasai environment is very apparent.

Maasai society has changed and is changing, yet its continuities remain clear and are strongly embedded in cultural practice. There are many signs of modernization in Maasailand today. Some Maasai now become rich from wheat farming and a wide variety of entrepreneurial activities, for example, rather than through accumulating cattle. And in some locations, especially in the vicinity of the larger national parks, the impact of tourism can be vividly seen. Moreover, much larger numbers of Maasai children are now attending primary schools than in the past. These changes are having, and will surely continue to have an increasing impact, but it has been the Maasai way to modernize on their own terms, taking what they can see a use for and discarding that which they do not require. In this way they have sought to preserve the core of their own social values and aspirations. To a greater extent than many other peoples in Eastern Africa, the Maasai today continue to make their own world in their own image. The continued survival of their society is rooted in the strength of their distinctive yet flexible culture. "*Meibor ng'eno lukunya,*" "the old have wisdom but so do those yet to come." Maasai have confidence in the ability of their society to endure.

Above: Maasai *moran* have their heads shaved by their mothers as part of their initiation ceremony.

Arhem, Kaj. *Pastoral Man In the Garden of Eden.* Uppsala: Institute for Cultural Anthropology, 1985.

Hinde, S.L. & H. *Last of the Maasai.* London: Heinemann, 1901.

Hollis, A.C. *The Maasai: Their Language and Folklore.* Oxford: Clarendon Press, 1905.

Kipury, Naomi. *Oral Literature of the Maasai.* Nairobi: Heinemann Educational Books, 1983.

Sankan, S. ole. *The Maasai.* Nairobi: Kenya Literature Bureau, 1979.

Spear, Thomas and Richard Waller, (eds). *Being Maasai: Ethnicity and Identity in East Africa.* London: James Currey; Athens OH: Ohio University Press; Dar es Salaam: Mkuki na Nyota; Nairobi: EAEP, 1993.

Spencer, Paul. *The Maasai of Matapato: A Study of Rituals of Rebellion.* Manchester: Manchester University Press for the International African Institute, 1988.

Bentsen, Cheryl. *Maasai Days.* New York: Anchor Books, 1991.

Mol, Father Frans. *Maa: A Dictionary of the Maa Language and Folklore.* Nairobi: Marketing & Publishing Ltd., 1978.

Saitoti, Tepelit ole. *The Worlds of a Maasai Warrior: An Autobiography.* New York: Random House, 1986.

Wagner-Glenn, Doris. *Searching for a Baby's Calabash: A Study of Arusha Maasai Fertility Songs as Crystallized Expression of General Cultural Values.* Ludwigsburg: Philipp Verlag, 1992.

Every effort has been made to trace all present copyright holders of the material used in this book, whether companies or individuals. Any omission is unintentional, and we will be pleased to correct errors in future editions of this book.

Text Acknowledgments:

The proverbs have been taken from a number of sources, including Kipury (1983), Sankan (1979) and Hollis (1905).

pp. 37, 41: Kipury, Naomi. *Oral Literature of the Maasai.* Nairobi: Heinemann Educational Books, 1983.

Picture Acknowledgments:

Adrian Arbib: Pages 4, 8, 11, 13, 14, 16, 19, 21, 22, 24, 26, 29, 30, 35, 41, 43, 44, 45, 47, 50, 55, 57.

Peter Jordan; Network Photographers: Pages 7, 38, 42, 58.

Roger Hutchins; Network

Photographers: Pages 33, 36.

Caroline Penn: Pages 12, 48.